Lexile:

LSU ⊠yes
SJB ☐yes
BL: 4.2
Pts: ι5

Tree Kangaroos

By Chuck Miller

Steadwell
Books

Raintree Steck-Vaughn Publishers

A Harcourt Company

Austin · New York

www.raintreesteckvaughn.com

ANIMALS OF THE RAIN FOREST

Published by Raintree Steck-Vaughn Publishers, an imprint of Steck-Vaughn Company.

Library of Congress Cataloging-in-Publication Data
Tree kangaroos/by Chuck Miller.
    p. cm.–(Animals of the rain forest)
    Includes bibliographical references (p. 31).
    ISBN 0-7398-5532-8
    1. Tree kangaroos—Juvenile literature. [1. Tree kangaroos. 2. Kangaroos.]
I. Title. II. Series.
QL737.M35 M538 2002
599.2'2—dc21   2001048969

Printed and bound in the United States of America
1 2 3 4 5 6 7 8 9 10 WZ 05 04 03 02

Produced by Compass Books

Photo Acknowledgments
Roger Williams Park Zoo, cover, title page, 12, 24; Lisa Dabek, 14, 26; William Betz, 6, 16. Wildlife Conservation Society, headquartered at the Bronx Zoo/Dennis DeMello, 8, 21. Root Resources/Kenneth Fink, 18, 28–29.

Editor: Bryon Cahill
Consultant: Sean Dolan

Content Consultant
Valerie Thompson
San Diego Zoo, California

This book supports the National Science Standards.

Contents

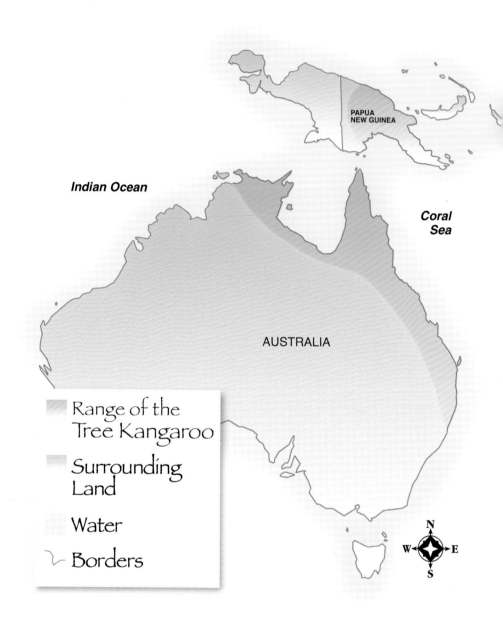

PAPUA
NEW GUINEA

Indian Ocean

Coral
Sea

AUSTRALIA

Range of the
Tree Kangaroo

Surrounding
Land

Water

Borders

N
W E
S

A Quick Look at Tree Kangaroos

What do tree kangaroos look like?
Tree kangaroos are small kangaroos with very long tails. Fur covers their whole bodies, except for their noses. Most tree kangaroos are brown, red, black, or gold.

Where do tree kangaroos live?
There are ten kinds of tree kangaroo. Two live in the rain forests of Australia. The other eight kinds live in New Guinea, a large island near Australia.

What do tree kangaroos eat?
Tree kangaroos eat mostly plants. They eat leaves, flowers, bark, and fruit. They sometimes eat insects, eggs, and young birds.

This tree kangaroo is resting on a branch in the rain forest.

Tree Kangaroos in the Rain Forest

Tree kangaroos are mammals. A mammal is a warm-blooded animal with a backbone. Female mammals give birth to live young and feed them with milk from their bodies. Warm-blooded animals have a body temperature that stays the same, no matter what the temperature is outside.

The scientific name for the tree kangaroo family is *Dendrolagus* (den-drah-LEG-es). This word means "tree rabbit" in Latin.

Tree kangaroos spend most of their lives in rain forest trees. A rain forest is a warm place where many different trees and plants grow close together, and a lot of rain falls. Rain forests have two seasons, a rainy season and a dry season. Little rain falls during the dry season.

▲ This female lives in a group with her young.

Where Do Tree Kangaroos Live?

Tree kangaroos live in the rain forests of northern Australia and New Guinea, which is a large island near Australia. Tree kangaroos are the only **arboreal** members of the kangaroo family. Arboreal animals live in trees.

Tree kangaroos usually live alone. Sometimes several females or females with young may live together. Each tree kangaroo has its own home range. They travel in this area to look for food. A male's home range is larger than a female's range. Sometimes a male's range may overlap with several females' ranges.

Males do not like being near other males. They will fight other males who come inside their range. Sometimes they fight to the death.

Tree kangaroos move very well among trees. To climb a tree, they wrap their arms loosely around its trunk. Then, they use their back feet to walk or hop up the trunk. Once in the trees, they walk or hop along branches. They may leap 30 feet (10 m) from tree to tree. They can even jump from a height of 65 feet (20 m) in a tree to the ground. They climb down trees tail first. When they are several feet above ground, they kick off from the trunk and twist in the air. This allows them to land standing up straight.

Trees in rain forests help tree kangaroos hide from **predators**. Predators are animals that hunt, kill, and eat other animals. Wild dogs hunt tree kangaroos. These predators have a hard time reaching tree kangaroos that are high in trees.

What Do Tree Kangaroos Look Like?

There are ten known kinds of tree kangaroo. Only two kinds live in Australia. The other eight kinds live in New Guinea. Scientists think there may be more kinds of tree kangaroos hiding in the thick forests that they have not found yet.

Different kinds of tree kangaroos are different sizes. Most are between 1.5 to 2.5 feet (50 to 80 cm) long. They weigh between 15 and 40 pounds (7 and 18 kg).

All tree kangaroos have very long tails. Tails can be up to 3 feet (90 cm) long. They use their tails to help them balance as they jump or climb. Unlike monkeys, tree kangaroos cannot use their tails to hold onto tree branches.

Fur covers all of a tree kangaroo's body, except for its nose. Tree kangaroo hair is different from the hair of most other mammals. It grows toward the back instead of toward the belly. The way the tree kangaroo's hair grows helps rainwater run off its body, instead of soaking into the fur.

Most tree kangaroos are brown or black. This camouflages them among rain forest trees. **Camouflage** is special coloring or patterns that help an animal blend in with its surroundings.

▲ **You can see the special fur coloring of these Matschie's tree kangaroos.**

Some tree kangaroos have other markings, too. They may have stripes, spots, and colorful stomachs or feet. For example, the species known as Matschie's tree kangaroo has dark brown fur on its back and light gold fur on its front.

▲ This tree kangaroo is using its sharp, curved claws to hold onto the branch.

How Are Tree Kangaroos Different from Other Kangaroos?

Tree kangaroos have special body parts that help them live in trees. Unlike kangaroos on the ground, tree kangaroos have long, strong arms. Tree kangaroos also have much shorter and wider legs than other kangaroos.

Pads of rough skin cover a tree kangaroo's hands and feet. This makes it easier for them to travel over rough tree bark. Tree kangaroos also have long, sharp, curved claws. They use the curved claws to grip branches.

Tree kangaroos have hands and feet made for life in the trees. Their wrists and ankles bend in different directions. This helps them grab leaves and branches. They can also move the fingers of their hands. They use the fingers to pick leaves.

A tree kangaroo's teeth are also suited for life in the trees. Unlike kangaroos that live on the ground, tree kangaroos have sharp teeth. They use these teeth to slice through leaves, tree bark, and nuts. Kangaroos that live on the ground have teeth that help them chew the grasses that they eat.

Tree kangaroos are the only kind of kangaroo that can walk. Kangaroos on the ground can only move both their feet at the same time and hop. Tree kangaroos can move their feet one at a time. They can walk or hop, if they want to.

This tree kangaroo is eating a piece of fruit.

What Tree Kangaroos Eat

Tree kangaroos are **omnivores**. Omnivores are animals that eat both plants and animals. Tree kangaroos eat mainly plants, such as leaves, nuts, bark, grass, flowers, and fruit. They may sometimes eat insects, bird eggs, or tiny chicks that have not left their nests.

Some tree kangaroos often eat tea leaves. Tea leaves contain tannin. Tannin makes things brown or reddish in color. Eating tannin gives some tree kangaroos their rich, colorful fur.

If tree kangaroos cannot find tannin to eat, their fur will lose some of its color. This happened to some tree kangaroos in zoos. When the zookeepers realized what had happened, they began feeding tea leaves to the tree kangaroos. The fur soon returned to its usual color.

This tree kangaroo has a special stomach to help digest the leaves that it eats.

Finding and Eating Food

Tree kangaroos are browsers. Browsers are animals that find food on the branches and flowers of trees and plants. Leaves, flowers, and fruit make up more than 80 percent of a tree kangaroo's diet.

Tree kangaroos spend only 10 percent to 50 percent of their time finding and eating food. They do not have to move far to find food. They eat the leaves from the trees in their home ranges. Scientists are not sure how large a home range the tree kangaroo has. It depends on the number of tree kangaroos living in one place and how much food there is.

Tree kangaroos have special stomachs that help them eat so many leaves. The stomachs contain **bacteria** that helps them **digest** the leaves quickly. Digest means to break down food so the body can use it. Bacteria are very small living creatures that cannot be seen except under a microscope.

Some tree kangaroos also spit their food back up after they have swallowed it. They chew their food a second time and swallow it again. This is called regurgitation. Regurgitation makes it easier for their stomachs to break down the leaves.

Young joeys like this one are pink and do not have fur.

A Tree Kangaroo's Life Cycle

Tree kangaroos are **marsupials**. Marsupials are mammals that carry their young in pockets on the front of their body. These pockets are called pouches.

Tree kangaroos do not have a special mating season. They can mate throughout the year. This is because there is always plenty of food in the rain forests where they live.

After mating, a young tree kangaroo grows inside the female for 39 to 45 days. Two to three days before giving birth, the female uses her tongue to clean out the inside of her pouch. Then, she gives birth.

A newborn tree kangaroo is called a **joey**. The joey is about the size of a quarter. It is pink, blind, and does not have fur.

Joeys

The first thing a joey does after being born is to crawl into its mother's pouch. The mother stays still, but does not help the joey. It holds onto its mother's fur and climbs. This trip takes about two minutes. If the joey falls, it will die.

Once inside the pouch, the mother feeds the joey milk from her body. This is called nursing. The joey drinks the milk and grows larger and stronger. It stays hidden in its mother's pouch for two months. The skin that makes up the pouch stretches to fit the growing joey. Then, it begins sticking its head out of the pouch and looking around.

At three months, the joey leaves its mother's pouch for short periods of time. But after eating, it climbs back into the pouch. It stays in the pouch for up to ten months.

A joey stays with its mother for a while after it leaves the pouch. It is fully grown in about 18 months. Then, it leaves to find its own home range.

Tree kangaroos can begin mating and producing young when they are 2 years old. Wild tree kangaroos live up to 15 years. Tree kangaroos in zoos have lived for 20 years.

This older joey can climb outside its mother's pouch for short periods of time.

These tree kangaroos are resting on the branches of rain forest trees.

A Tree Kangaroo's Day

Some tree kangaroos move around mostly during the day. Other kinds of tree kangaroos move around mostly at night.

Tree kangaroos are not very active animals. They spend more than half of their time sleeping. They sleep curled up in the branches of whatever tree they happen to be in at the time.

It is easiest to see tree kangaroos during the day when they are sleeping. This is because tree kangaroos move around in the trees at night to hide from predators and each other. But during the day, many tree kangaroos sleep in thick tree branches near the ground.

For a short time each day, tree kangaroos **groom** themselves. Groom means to clean oneself. Tree kangaroos lick themselves and use a special toe on their back feet to clean their fur. The toe helps them pick bugs and other things out of their fur.

The rest of a tree kangaroo's day is spent slowly traveling through rain forest trees. While doing this, they look for food and stop often to rest. Some tree kangaroos climb down trees to look for food on the rain forest floor.

Tree kangaroos like this one are an endangered species.

The Future of Tree Kangaroos

There were once other kinds of tree kangaroos. Scientists know this because they found a fossil of a kind of tree kangaroo that does not exist anymore. Fossils are the remains or imprints, such as footprints, left by animals that lived long ago. The fossil showed that **extinct** tree kangaroos were up to three times larger than the ones living now. Extinct means there are no animals of that kind left alive in the wild.

Today, some kinds of tree kangaroos are **endangered**. Endangered refers to a species or kind of animal that may become extinct. Scientists think there are only about 2,000 tree kangaroos left in the wild.

▲ These scientists are putting a special radio on this tree kangaroo so they can track it.

What Will Happen to Tree Kangaroos?

Tree kangaroos are endangered because they are losing their **habitat**. The rain forests of Australia and New Guinea are disappearing. People are cutting down trees to make room for new homes and farms. They are also selling the wood from trees. Tree kangaroos need rain

Like all kangaroos, tree kangaroos are called by different names. Female kangaroos are called flyers. Males are known as boomers. A mob is the name for a group of kangaroos.

forest trees to live in. Tree kangaroos do not like to move very far from their habitats. They will stay close to the land where the trees once were. This puts them in danger.

Some people who live near rain forests hunt tree kangaroos. These people can easily catch tree kangaroos in fallen trees and then cook and eat them. They think tree kangaroo meat tastes good.

Tree kangaroos try to cross roads to move around their home ranges. When they do this, they may be hit and killed by a car.

Most people believe the best way to keep tree kangaroos from becoming extinct is to save rain forests. In rain forests, tree kangaroos can hide from predators. Some people are working to make laws against hunting tree kangaroos. This will help keep tree kangaroos alive in their rain forest habitats in the future.

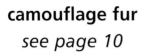

camouflage fur
see page 10

long tail
see page 9

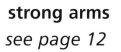

strong arms
see page 12

sharp claws
see page 13

Glossary

arboreal (ar-BOR-ee-ul)—living mainly in trees

bacteria (bak-TEAR-ee-uh)—tiny living creatures that cannot be seen without a microscope

camouflage (KAM-o-flaj)—colors, shapes, and patterns that make something blend in with its background

digest (dye-JEST)—to break down food so the body can use it

endangered (en-DAYN-jurd)—a species or kind of animal that is almost extinct

extinct (ek-STINKT)—a species that has died out

groom (GROOM)—to clean one's body or another animal's body

habitat (HAB-i-tat)—the place where an animal or plant usually lives

joey (JOE-ee)—a young tree kangaroo

marsupials (mahr-SOUP-ee-uhls)—mammals that carry their young in a pouch on the front of their body

omnivores (AHM-nee-vohrs)—animals that eat both plants and animals

predators (PRED-uh-turs)—animals that hunt other animals for food

Internet Sites

Animals of the Rain Forest: Tree Kangaroo
www.animalsoftherainforest.com/
    treekangaroo.htm

The Tree Kangaroo and Mammal Group
www.herbertonss.qld.edu.au/treekangaroo/
    about.html

Useful Address

The Tree Kangaroo and Mammal Group Inc.
P.O. Box 1409
Atherton, Qld 4833
Australia

Books to Read

Crewe, Sabrina. *The Kangaroo.* Austin, TX:
    Steck-Vaughn, 1997.

Knight, Tim. *Journey into the Rainforest.* London:
    Oxford University's Children's Books, 2001.

Index